LETTER FROM ULSTER
& THE HUGO POEMS

LETTER FROM ULSTER
&
THE HUGO POEMS

E. A. Markham

LITTLEWOOD ARC
1993

Published by Littlewood Arc
Nanholme Mill, Shaw Wood Road,
Todmorden, Lancs. OL14 6DA.

Design by Tony Ward
Printed by Arc & Throstle Press
Nanholme Mill, Todmorden, Lancs.
Typeset by Anne Lister Typesetting
Beacon Business Centre, Halifax.

ISBN 0 946407 88 6

Acknowledgements are due to the
following journals in which some of
these poems have previously appeared:
*Agenda, Ambit, The North, Outposts,
The PBS Anthology (1990),
Poetry Durham, Poetry Ireland Review,
Poetry Review, rhinoceros, Stand, Verse.*
Anthologies: *Sing Freedom,* Faber;
Hinterland, Bloodaxe; *Hugo Versus
Montserrat,* Linda Lee Books, and on the
Bluefoot Cassettes (1990). Some have
been broadcast on BBC Radio Four,
Radio Ulster and Radio Sheffield. In 1991
Hearing Eye brought out a pamphlet of
Maurice V's Dido.

The publishers acknowledge financial
assistance from Yorkshire and
Humberside Arts Board and North West
Arts Board.

For Angela and Bob Welch

CONTENTS

PART ONE: LETTER FROM ULSTER

Letter from Ulster
Hinterland / 11
Island / 13
I'm looking through Glass,
    I'm tasting Poison / 15
Letter from Ulster / 17

Nostalgia
J'accuse / 37
A Poem about a Savant . . . / 39
On explaining the Results
    of the Race to your Mother / 41
Death in the Family, 1988 / 42
A Little Bit of our Past / 46
And for Some Reason . . . / 48
A Date on the Calendar / 50

Lines, Ancient & Modern
Maurice V.'s Dido / 55
A Hundred Lines / 67
Letter to Kate / 73
To dance with Desmond Tutu / 75
War Casualty / 77

PART TWO: THE HUGO POEMS

Here we go again / 81
Preachers, Preachers / 83
Major Browne's Library, Montserrat / 85
Kevin's Message to Montserrat / 88
Hugo Fallout / 89

1
Letter from Ulster

Hinterland

The dreams are wet. Tonight rain
In Portrush, home of two months. I wake
To seagulls, accept the logic
Of dream and unpack the cases: life
Will be here near Malin Head –
Like Rockall, an outpost on the weathermap.
I rehearse a prayer to my travelling
Relic, a grandmother sure to exact,
Like other gods, penance for this blasphemy.
The first wet dream was not the joke
Schoolboys brag about, but fear
Of stretching out a foot from Montserrat
And falling into sea. In France, in Germany,
In spray-white Sweden the first stumble
Across a street turned ground to water
With waves of language rearing up
To lift you out of depth. Lucky
You didn't unpack – though the cases now
Are full, wares and gifts outdated,
And your fresh discoveries changing shape
And colour like your photograph.
Another day in Portrush: wind and rain.
There is security in this, part
Of the hinterland of an experience
Still to be reclaimed. New Guinea
Was too fabled, generous in its reprieve:
A threat – its gift too close to dreams
For waking comfort. London was like a parents'
Home from which to rebel. Now here, on the edge
Of the edge, the sea hurling defiance
At old, at new gods, I pray to the familiar
In my suitcase, in my head: I have

Explored the world, tasted its strangeness,
Resisted and colluded out of strength,
Out of weakness, failed to colonize it
With family tongue or name. Are you pleased
Secretly, with a frown pulling down on relief?
The treasures I carry in my head fail
To match the refuse in my case.
But it will do, and the dreams tonight
To douse a fear, will perhaps be wet.

Island

1

A convenient image only
to help you, my friend, my darling,
my destroyer – and talking of destroyers,
white and splendid on the sea,
like forbidden triumphs of an early
culture, hermaphroditic in their promise,
Ladies growing erect with guns – enough.
Enough to bring the blush to past lovers.

2

Do not mock the poverty of our invasion,
mis-spelled placards and voices which parody
sound, thanks to your friends – so powerful
they need no uniforms – who have held us
from the presence. Don't be generous;
do not arrange a delegation through
the cordon. You know what's written there.
My love, you know also, most of these wrecks
which disturb your peace, are sunk. Unsafely.

3

"He survived the plane-crash."
These are the ones who didn't,
and have torn through the skim
of our life to remind us
of the myth. The day your logic
broke and you stuck it together
and no crack showed through the sentence,
is being remembered, is being lived.
Those for whom cracks were never mended
are here, bits of them trying to assemble

bits of you they care to claim. They attack —
guns, bombs, badverbs — evacuated arguments.
On the horizon, another island afloat, Ah,
in a sea of salt: a line,
a rope, a plan of rescue:
how best to invade?

I'm looking through Glass, I'm tasting Poison

1

I'm searching, searching for a first line
as if chained to the bed, unthinking you . . .
I'm washing the bottoms of milk bottles, prior to fridge.
I'm thinking of timeless gestures – the cat darting in, out
as the door ends centuries of waiting.
These memories mist the glass too easily:
Better to look through it, and think of others tasting poison.

2

And as I talk to myself again through you,
knowing you're unlikely to have names and faces
I imagine; or, in a darkened theatre
a blur from up here, behind lights –
there is no need to play it safe, to match
halves for the perfect fit tonight.
So, behind glass, I plunge into Sahara. I swim.

3

I am blind, of course, the glass
is a trick of sight. Eyes
glaze from footage on the assembly line
like the years passing in stanzas, inches from my face,
regiments of maimed, the undead to make me see.
I see: then how better to use this magic
to quell let's call them furies, too much explained?

4

Let's say there is grief, or something less
too tempting to indulge. Let's say
on a body that side of glass, a scar
reforms into the healing smile of Second Best.
How can you retain faith in the old storms,
the kind raging in the head, flooding
your own country, silting its river?

5

I lower my guard as if you're here beside me:
we've hung the pictures, reordered the room
for living. Through the window your fingers bloom
like flowers new to my vocabulary. The glow
of your voice outliving the piano flickers
what might have been . . . might have been.
The rest is silly. The drink is funny.

6

I lower my guard as if you're here beside me –
the pretence of talking in public dropped –
the fart, in pride, restrained as you come in to tease
flowers new to my vocabulary into season,
far from assembly-line of days to remember days
to regret. And we vow, don't we, to recover what is ours
by exxing out those lines about glass and poison.

Letter from Ulster

for Mimijune

1

I'm 300 years old;
the partner arrives and is shown into
the drawing-room where someone makes her comfortable.
She is, we think, 40 years early.
The boy sits in an upstairs room, his back
to the window, typewriter on the bed
two-finger tapping a scene from the house
next-door – a young girl folded in the arms
of a man, open curtains with promise
that travel from St. Caesare[1] to Ladbroke Grove
might fulfil. Neither typist nor writer he turns
too late, the curtains are closed.
Downstairs, mother entertains an in-law 40 years early
with scenes from a life more real than this:
the drawing-room floor is freshly polished, smell
of wax like flowers from the garden toasting
in the sun. Wasps' nests have been removed
from gable and gallery, lizards and other irritants
dealt with by someone unseen who nurses
a better version of this house. Look out
of the window – through glass panes, a bridal
present for the young mother never to shed
hint of girlishness in the crossing – glass panes,
first on this side of the island –
at grapes with a hint of salt, though the sea,
as you see – so calm today, how could we be sick? –
is distant… ah. But will you take
ginger beer or coconut juice with ice? Downstairs,
in this recent house imposed on other houses where occupants
vanish in mid-sentence leaving you unsure of tricks
being played – downstairs, brothers talk of an election

17

coming up, promises that must be made
to us here in England, to us in South Africa,
to us everywhere as price of the vote. (Old Professeur
Croissant used to say in class: if you must lie,
lie intelligently. If you must, sell yourself
dearly, a play on words too risky for parents born
before our time.) Excluded from the couple
behind their curtain and from the brothers' debate
– and from what else? – I plead
unreadiness to meet a partner, years early.

2

Dear X,

They call it confidence to offer
false starts to an intimate this late
in the game, but what if no better version comes? . . .
though this stand colludes, perhaps, with failure.
So, dear X, skip these lines of self-
regard, worn apologies
for omission, unreadiness, these practised
ways of shoring *Self.* To you, to others
who have turned up early, these games
irritate; they bore. Mock the time
with family growing into the real thing.
Stray postcards confirm your luck, you've escaped
the jokes – remember when Pullar and Parkhouse[2]
were in contention to open the batting for England? –
that no one understands. That off our chests – Oh chest! –
safe to revert to the present with a letter
from Ulster. Scenes of local colour
won't do the trick – too much blood
under the lamp-posts, joke. 300 years seems
a short time to manage a life cleansed
of its past yet love-propelled;
but my time-creditor comes like an assistant
at the bank and says, enough: others,
who are not bright, manage it in the slot
allotted. Think of lives you have put
on hold by slowing things to this pace. Your drawing-
room partner, distanced now by – whom? – a stand-in
daughter, has outlived the house, the fantasy.
Brothers, far from downstairs, answering to other
cares protect themselves from new "South Africas"
(child and wife and self-abuses, biologies with your name

on). And they go out to vote. And what, pray,
of that early couple behind the curtain?
But I promised you relief from a letter
too stiff to compel reading between
the lines. A limp letter, then, and addressed
to someone, on another continent, not tempted
to read between our lines.

Dear Jim & Elisabeth,

This is not the letter, I know. I'll write
at the weekend to thank you for Canada
(lovely present, unspoilt, where will I put it?)
for good times remembered, the walk through the ravine
that beautiful Sunday with Elisabeth (we're adults now,
no Atwood childhood fears. Remember Cat's Eye?)
Thanks for the hospitality, the space . . .
But first, let me clear my mind a bit
as resolution ebbs on this Coleraine-Belfast train.
Cutting it fine, as always, I crash the guardsman's
van, pleased, no seconds today, to spare –
and I'm missing a package, a bag – left
in the taxi, snatched on the steps? the race
over foot-bridge, messy: students pouring the other way
helped when the straps broke: white bag
with books, green bag MADE IN CANADA, my change
of clothing, a white top, for Belfast,
after a bath – fresh for the late-night studio.

I'm in the guard's van. Maybe he thinks:
they need longer to recover breath
than men in our parts, all that running and jumping
on television. He makes small allowances
for this puffing race and settles a little more

in his skin. Today, bag-snatched, I see no reason
to take better care of his feelings than he does.
I rise to the occasion (it's a coarse time
but we'll outwit it) and see hoardes cross the bridge,
motorcycle-helmeted, moll-painted, struggling
to don white Westing House gear and I . . . check myself in time.

Dear Elisabeth & Jim

3

A government-suited man behind a desk: to show
he's human or to ease the tension, makes a joke
(not about the Chinese lady at Dhu Varren
railway station, though that comes to mind) . . . Which of us
will act this man's throwaway line
and end up in the papers? And here we are coming out
of the film of the book, telling friends over a pizza
how the cut-price Bogart got it wrong. Across the road
filmed, too, in drizzle your tail lights a cigarette in the doorway. See!
Better to talk about the railway clock in Portrush Havishamed
at 11.25 encouraging old bachelors
to rewrite their history as literature.
I've caught the bug. Let me read you
the menu of the Chinese restaurant
(Lower Main Street) as a poem . . .

You're right, my love. The act
degenerates, distraction/from a life
we might have lived/points
to an analyst

behind this glimpse of happiness,
behind this naked breast, voices
of old men unscramble/made human
by translation, their toothless lives no longer
excluding from the feast of family feeling
those not dressed for table:
the rhubarb chorus (something to rhyme with table?
to swat the buzzing chorus?)
makes you pause and turn away/careful
not to repel the naked breast/I say

having lost the prize:
I will add some years to mine

till it comes around next time.

4

Meanwhile enter Horace
our Interlude, pink
ribbon in his hair, pink
shoe-lace in his memory-
pocket for a daughter
ever pink and beautiful:
Derringer's the name
name o'th'game, our Shaman
restored to humour.
Wars & roaming have dis-
tempered, slack-minded
this lover of Peace, stiff-
limping into action.
He appears on cue
against the tide of Comanche Cheyenne Sioux[3]
back to you (he can do
the Ali shuffle, too!):
now at his piano miming
the old tunes. *In The Mood
& If I Give My Heart To You* . .
(10,000 at Salamis, more at Zama[4]
negotiations between the generals having failed)
Will You Handle It With Care..?
He is not blind, he outwits
doctors and family, this Special
Envoy to Europa, bringing *shhh*
(from St. Caesare, off
your map, don't look now)
Bustcrumvrst Mvst
Peace in his language,
in this or that language:
Messenger Horace broken-
toothed on his diet of phrases

WIR HABEN[5] (try this one)
UNS MIT NACHBARN ÜBER DIE
BENÜTZUNG DES GARTENS ARRANGIERT
no pillow-talk now to Merles
& Sadies of Coderington
to Cathy and Sharon of Ealing and Edmonton.
But public lament for
Hrothvitha Hrothvitha[6]
stage-wife and daughter
petals in the slaughter
to divert you from comfort,
from solemnity. And so –
May you never lack for caress
May your lover be left-
                          handed and relentless
May Sally paint your door in bright colours
May you be the pick of your brothers
and so on and so on *Hrothvitha*
Hrothvitha a name no one claims for
these Sisters and Mothers.

Brokentoothed fly-
opened Horace ends
with a memory that he sings
unaccompanied, his own melody, pink-
ribboned melody, his
something-hearted melody, his
broken-charted melody, his

broken-hearted melody . . .

5

Puck
Just a note, darling;
I've had to explain you
appropriate you (for Mimijune &
Julieblossom) to see how you'd run:
Ama Ata Aidoo,
tripple A.
b. Ghana, 1939, playwright,
novelist, etc. Address Zimbabwe
(see essay by Innes,
Lyn of Canterbury.) So,
you were my near-choice
for the Chair
to prick these Oberons,
these Titanias (immune with collars)
and constituencies cross-
border (swing high, swing low . . .)
with a virus of compassion
as they learn to betray your name
in a common accent:
Ama Ata Aidoo
Chairperson to this Conference
not allowed
(by a daughter of Ghana,
sister of Zimbabwe)
to break up
on this rock of malespeak
solid through the ages.

Mimijune, Julieblossom.
In the wings. My favourite things.

6

I wake up howling: murder
has become easy to the long-lived. I'm committing
it again. The pistol in the pants
slugs a consenting victim
in the crotch. I do not have Aids,
I say. But the victim dies. Everywhere
it gets easier to kill. (And the coward
says: let me turn away from the loved one
before we wake.) Meanwhile the years
turn against us. Solutions elude us.
How long, O Lord, is this string spun
from vanity, how long
will the earth sustain it?

Dear John & Joan,

(lacking courage
for today again on the television, an outrage
occurs – the plumber, shop-assistant outguesses
me in the quiz of what I call my subject.
Pride must be recovered before approach
to another with intent.
Lacking courage like
the blind man at Sheffield Railway Station
charging down the stairs, scattering passengers;
like getting on with a former life;
like dying early, I turn
to another, slack letter, my darling,
and mild abuse of Canada. In lieu of lovers'
cards, the codes uncracked in the post,
I blame the time, I blame the place.)

My mispronunciations of Agincourt[7] were deliberate.
I, too, live in Henry V country only when abroad.
Just a letter from Ulster to thank you for Canada,
big country, clean accent, etc... And about me?
O, fun times in Ballymena, Ballymoney. Limavady.
Riding the middle of the train one day (not the first
carriage or the last, making it safe, like a New Yorker
story shorn of beginning and end) the second smoker
lights up, the third girl-farmer splotches mud on my seat:
I like it, folks, the wild North, I'm not too late
for the rush. Later, I'll play myself in Hollywood.
But competition is stiff for the films. At audition
near Portrush (the place where the train, programmed
to leave late, surprises you one day by being early)
I rated one line, the privileged extra . . .
The time is evening, the place Dhu Varren, the train
not running. A bus – looking like a bus – pulls up
and rail-passengers get on. Except for the Chinese
lady hovering, holding out. "There's no train today",
the conductor treads on my cue, with no result.
The language-student wants a playback. So pointing
to UNIVERSITY bus, idling, he announces: THIS IS
THE TRAIN. This, a week after events at Tiananmen
Square where nobody died. This "train" an English
joke in Ireland?

Old men used to say: stones grow.
Men at home grew grey on such evidence.
No one thought of land-erosion. But the same men say:
cut me and I bleed, auditioning for Shylock;
trapped here, I die. Ah, if they thought of land-erosion
they would find ways out of this, with the family intact.
I stand accused of lengthening moments
into string, as if that were in short supply
in the average life.

O yes, I meant to say, they sent me
a list of 24 poets, names and addresses,
colleagues at the HARBOURFRONT⁸, for a week. Telephone
numbers, too. How open. How good. Canada.

Mimijune, Julieblossom,

The change of clothing, the white top
reclaimed at home in Portrush, my oversight,
made me see how rash to write too soon
a letter from Ulster, to write to you
in innocence. Instead, the white top,
stolen on the road from London to Sheffield,
delays the letter. But what of you?

Portrush: Fragments from the Journal

I

Land, I think, though only just.
Gales from Iceland whistle through the caravel.
The seas, enraged at this obstruction threaten,
relent and come again, green-backed with teeth
straining from the world of myth. Some say
these monsters will not be ridden; these are tales
of desperate men far from home. Next will come
the triumph of supping with the devil
without the long spoon; and that will grant your wish
of keeping good folk at home.

II

Then the land shrank back in a terrible roar
As the green-backed, white-teethed
Mass made for the shore
Spitting sea-pebbles with venom
Like a line of snipers compelling
You to yield. This zealot's canon
Bends you down, crouches you in mime
Of humans in drink, each desperado
– And we have all been there in time –
Fantasising a railway-station pub at Portrush.
And some say the King of Spain
Has now laid claim to Portrush.
But on to the real El Dorado round
The promontory, our university teeming,
Its band of natives browned
By no sun, and like the bless'd of the old
World, well-proportioned, except for webbed
Feet and tendency to walk backwards in leave-taking[9]. Gold
Is our currency, though rival discovery

Of men with breasts or bird or fish aspect
Still serves, if not national recovery
Or fixing the State plumbing,
To head off ruin and the Tower. The *cassique*[10]
In chains, must fear our Second Coming.

III

Too dangerous to say what you've found.
The sealed envelope (why should this be found?)
Would explain all should we suffer mishap.
A new god of hail descends like an icecap
Sneezing; unkind to flesh and eyeglass. Wind & rain
(And faulty instruments) make it hard to retain
Our humour. Exploring's no longer the sum
Of delights promised when the journey was begun.
Wet with indignity, men think this train
Of misery that brought them here, the same
That through Law of Averages, if not prayer,
Must lug back to those early stations of hope. Fair's fair.
In time a train train stops unscheduled at Portrush
Where the spirits have not been propitiated. Portrush
Is a rooftop vandal hurling down slate at your feet
Daring you to assume safe passage to Main St.
You get home bleeding, fire-water the graze
and much else; relent, and sit down to write the day's
Journal when the light blows out.
I'm sitting in the dark; there are Christians about.

1 **St. Caesare:** Imaginary island off the coast of Montserrat in the Caribbean.

2 **Pullar and Parkhouse:** In the late 50s, early 60s, England cricket selectors cast about for opening batsmen who could give solidarity to the innings. Of the two in contention here, Pullar had some success against West Indies in 1959.

3 **Comanche Cheyenne Sioux:** Horace is moving *against* the trend, pushing back the damage. From about AD 1600, when enough Europeans were established on the east coast of America with superior weapons, the Indians were driven westwards into the territory of westerly neighbours. The succession of great battles – between the Chippewa and the Sioux – at Mille Lacs in the 17th century; at Elk River in the 18th and at Cross Lake in 1800, have become part of our myth. In the 19th century, the buffalo gone, the pressure westwards continuing, the defeated Sioux pushed the Cheyenne (and others) further west. The Cheyenne eventually drove the Comanche back towards Mexico.

4 **Salamis and Zama:** The naval battle at Salamis between the Greeks and the Persians (Sept. 480 BC) led to a notable Greek victory and heavy casualties. At Zama (Oct-Nov. 202 BC) the Second Punic War ended with Scipio Africanus overcoming the Carthaginians under Hannibal. The entire Carthaginian army of 35,000 was killed or captured, though Hannibal escaped. His infantry was semi-trained and his elephants confused by Scipio's blast of trumpets and horns along the whole length of his line. Also, by 202, Hannibal had had 16 years of continuous high-command.

5 **WIR HABEN...:** We've come to an arrangement with the neighbours about the use of the garden.

6 **Hrothvitha:** 10th century Saxon nun who wrote plays – generally with a Christian subject – in the style of Terence.

7 **Agincourt:** The Canadian town with an English pronunciation.

8   **HARBOURFRONT:** Toronto. Certainly, the most splendidly-organized poetry reading event in the west. Presided over by Greg Gatenby.

9   **tendency to walk backwards in leave-taking:** An observation first made by Dr. Richard Bradford of Portrush, in conversation.

10 **Cassique:** Local ruler in the Americas during the time of conquest, often roughly treated at the hands of the Colóns and the Raleighs . . .

Nostalgia

J'accuse

We did all the right things
Worked all the week
Treated the servants well
Added to the house, praised
Those spirits who didn't embarrass us.

Some turned cane into sugar,
Into rum: we were lucky
With cotton. And at night
When the hill-side god deserted
Our stone foundations and spare rooms,

And set the animal pound braying,
And the kerosene lamp flickering,
We recited the old stories
Of hurricanes fought in these rooms
With bibles white and black

Through to a safe morning.
But what to do about gods
Gone missing, asking forgiveness
From this or that far land,
Their protection

Like the mosquito-net, an upside-
Down catch for fish, a mockery,
As the days wear their night-
Games, servant and mistress standing in
Remagicking the house

As cassava-box melts into
Coffin, black against white

Poison (and the carpenter, maker
of box and coffin, at rest, somewhere,
Innocent)? We did the right thing

For we had paid already
With children in the ground,
And men who hadn't written,
And men who repaired the wrong house.
Now, long after we're gone, a ship

Crashes into our mountain,
Its people uninvited, reclaiming
Cassava boxes, soon to be blessed.
Hard to found a village, even now,
With so much sacrifice.

A Poem about a Savant, a Sister & a Person very grand at a
Function who must first look around the Room for Someone
more important to talk to, and then relent.

He was the Stapleton who matured
like cheese which reminds you of something else
into a Character the village loved
to offer to strangers as evidence

of a sophisticated palate. Old Stapleton
talked calmly of violence and death
unlike the preacher, to banish both as a daily fear
without condemning the island to something folksy.

He preserved the risk that he could do worse
if he tried, to confirm the family's dread
of *savant* as something others called strange
in whispers or with after-dinner relish.

Though for a sister, visiting,
how irksome this man without family
making death 'n violence a party piece, neighbours
she'd kept at bay by effort in a life

ministering to others! And here they are together
at a function, approached by a person very grand,
contrition on his face. And yes, women
are like wives to public men at times like these.

Old Stapleton tells the story of his sister's
daughter when young, helping to pull weeds
from the driveway, from the garden: why then
is she crying, the happy child? Those flowers

in an adult hand, though green, have done no harm,
and calling them names won't make it better.
This story of death and violence in the family
softens the sister and intrigues a person very grand.

On explaining the Result of the Race
to your Mother

Her eyes are bad; you can't take refuge
in that: her sons erect on the podium
receiving medals for running and jumping
have to be acknowledged. Why *them,* you think,
with a rash of jealousy lotioned
into something more presentable: *they*
chasing the wind, leaping the bar, have stretched
your mind, too, past comfort. So why not *us,* nearer
home, greyer, trailing in another pack but clutching
goodies made visible by our words? The old arguments
are too heavy for mind alone to shift. Three sons
(not strangers), same face, accent, each with a national
anthem not her own: the mother's eyes
see past this snub. There were times, it's true,
when men left home to build in foreign
lands, and scattered seed where no one knew.
A few decades reapprenticed to the world and we've shifted
view on what's good and not good to know: there are
no bastards in this family now grown large
by claiming its own. But the flags
held aloft by children fingering medals
have nothing left of our cloth: will this extend
the emergency order of exile? A memory
fogs like cloud over those factories, farms unkind
to animals which bring protesters out on the street.
Ah yes. But remember, the sky over cruelty
can be blue: (so many flags show good weather!)
Let's watch the television; your distant sons
smile and wave. Daughters now. More flags. Gold
hung from necks more precious than the rest. And let's
not look at one another while we're being honoured.

41

Death in the Family, 1988
after a father, for a mother

1
thinking about my mother, thinking
about a joke she might have told, setting
the scene to make it seem

unforced . . . The butcher's shop in Ladbroke Grove in the 50s
was a tough audition for one
unaccustomed to playing the messenger, or head of the family:

there, weighing need and status –
heads and tails and innards ruled out;
dead flesh to be cleaned ruled out –

bits of chicken, then, one bit for each member
for this is England and exile made you measure
not only the weight of glances and words thrown across the street

but what you ate
and how much warmth you let into the air around you:
five bits of chicken, please.

The telephone rang and rang and guilty
to be caught at this after 30 years
I learnt of a death in the family.

I listened to what accompanies news of death in the family,
and promised to pass it on,
and agreed how it should be passed on

And I checked myself for signs of afterlife.
The bath this morning to greet the world
seemed right; panic about bills unpaid began to subside.

The damp-marks in my room still sent the same message. REPAIR ME.
Estrangement from a too-dear friend, her beauty flawed
in wanting to embrace the cheat in you –

seems less like logic now, less
like damp marks on walls, less like
your shift within the world.

For now, my son, a quiet hand has removed
a shelter that was useful, that was kind (why
aren't there hurricanes, revolutions, strange happenings as in *Lear?*)

There is nothing between you and the last appeal:
you are pressed against the barricades; the space
which cushioned till today, is occupied by you now:

you can't decline it, choice remains
but like a shadow to your *self*
like the two-headed coin you toss without protest: you must take

the weight of others
who will not grant breathing space
who look at you as fixture, always there

who are impatient, reckless, sporadic in their need
who want sometimes to fail – to check if you are real
who do and do not wish to take your place

and I go to the bathroom and find that things work much the same
and I suspect countries on the map are where we left them
and I welcome the shy, unexpected, prod of hunger . . .

2
I think back to that 50s scene
the lady (wife, long-distanced, to the one
whose death is now reported: we will tell her, we've discussed it)

losing her tongue, like a novice, at this butcher's shrine
(she knew a husband's commandments would be obeyed).
Later, it was possible, when chicken came in bits –

not that they came in bits, you understand: that was
the joke that never worked – later, in another part of town
when she had grown attuned to shopping

(but not to taking insides from dead meat)
she developed ways of withstanding
the pressure of the queue – and of honing her joke.

Five pieces not because there were five in the family
– there were five in the family –
but because in this England you had to count things differently.

From this they understood much
that she had not intended:
even the jokes here set you back.

Another failure, the family, growing tired of wings
made their own jokes of being tired of wings:
five *legs* seemed so difficult to be at ease with . . .

Thinking back to what produced five legs
she saw two of her mother's chickens *and a half.*
The horror of the half made her think

44

in this long-frozen land
where the family, itself a half of something never planned,
this was a joke all would understand:

so she asked for *five* pieces from two chickens
and a lame one; and the man with blood on him laughed . . .
When she moved house again the other man laughed.

A Little Bit of our Past . . .
for Olive and Jessica

Here's a bone under glass, and reproductions
of birds long vanished known to ancestors
who wouldn't have imagined us. Other exhibits show
birth, marriage and death, their dry riverbed
of history, moistening with recognition
that the cultivated areas where we live
are not far from the source. Closer still,
the soundtrack lifelike, the dress modern, a mother
beating her son with inherited skills
some in our midst claim to possess.

The mother – call her Olive, call her Jessica –
a petite, kind woman you'd treasure
as a friend, asks you to witness her problem.
This is no big Momma beating up on the boy,
but a priestess of manners ordained to prevent
Satan re-entering the family as an animal.
He so rude he drive you to distraction.
Here she is all dressed up and ready to go out,
he not just making her late he spoiling her style, daring
her to use whip as if she's some marketwoman
anxious to parade herself in public. What to do now?
She don't even have a strap to teach the boy a lesson.
So she have to fold up her little fists into a ball
and shut her eyes tight not to see as she thump him up;
and he hurt her hand, you know?
And now the exertion make her hot; she flush, she have
to go change her blouse again, and sprinkle
a little water on her skin to cool it down –
and don't talk to her about shame and humiliation and feeling small:
You know something just spring loose inside her head

which make her mad. The boy lips curl up like a challenge
from on high, *and it make her mad!*
And you know she can't even remember if he start to throw
back words at her, but she hearing them.
The more she hit and cuff, the more she bathing him in licks,
she feeling the blows, she taking *Language* in exchange
that lash and sting and curl her up; she feel
those sudden jets of steam that catch you from the kettle, bruising her.
The way he standing she knows the boy still aiming
words at his mother as if this is boxing-
ring, and he squaring up against his equal.
And he jabbing her with rudeness like
he is big man already playing with woman.
And if you witness such a scene no one could say
she don't have duty as a Christian and a woman
to teach him manners –
it's her cross to bear and everyone must suffer in this life.

And Maisie used to say: you got to beat them till
they say sorry and they mean it,
which is not a lot to ask of people who are not beasts of the field:
some say you have to start early
before they turn into man like the men already in your life,
ready to walk all over woman and cause trouble in the land,
and, you know, the sorts of arguments that go with that.
But child, I don't believe it doing any good,
whether you beat him in his Sunday clothes
or on the nakedness too raw and proud for comfort now,
is you going suffer pain, till they relieve you.
For licks not going to stop woman liking him
which is what you fear and hope;
and in the end you tired and beaten –
and you compromise and ask the boy the hurtful question.
You look him in the eye and say: why it is you want to kill me so?
And if I tell you that the child so rude and stubborn
he refuse even to answer, you going say I lie!

And for Some Reason . . .

And for some reason they called him Horace
which was lucky as his condition couldn't be blamed
without malice on any lost member of the family;
though 'Horace' struck a note which sounded fine
as if the mouths of aunts and grannies trained to it
were conscious that no outside instrument kept them company:
let's pretend we're in another country and we are foreign
and what you're hearing is your own music and laughter.

And for some reason this pause in our lives
just out of earshot, out of vision of your company, keeps us busy
filling in the background of a canvas too huge
for a man the wrong size since his birth.
Bright and rude he was born to bear loads, run errands
in his head and leave the muscles free for mischief.
Let's say he did all this, another champion of the world,
and in retirement now mocks us toning up his portrait.

The hidden pictures show he ruled the house by cunning
and read books in gibberish whose medicines then failed him,
and while abroad married of their women
more than is good for men of these parts; and was caught
and released, damaged in ways closed to fathers and uncles
except in dream, their jumbies meeting, like village elders for censure;
and for some reason we were unlucky with others in the family
not called Horace; so why not call him Horace?

Let's say – do you blame us? – he fell at the fence, was shot in the back;
let's say he's had a good war, but liberated
the wrong country, confusing family and friends:
our natural athlete pinned to his flesh blinks, blinks

to show a life after life, winks at old men from the village
who missed all the tricks save to pallaver
whether the boy was returned from abroad too soon; and, yes,
for some reason women and girls of the house keen his name.

A Date on the Calendar

The days come and go.
I lurch this way and that
through my Amazonian
exile, dripping

hallucinating. I get up,
peel away nightrags,
find something dry,
uncontaminated

and collapse again.
Dreams come in shoals,
jealous of body's treat
to something special;

or to collude with brain
that minutes not days
break these spasms
of measurement.

I dream a man
remote from us –
a white farmer, say,
somewhere in Africa,

or Wyoming –
calls on a lady
of my acquaintance. She buys
(or sells or declines)

a ticket for a function.
She marks the date
on the calendar. Ah,
the rest is forgotten.

I am travelling down
Orinoco, hacking through
Yanamami country. Centuries
or inches. Time to take stock.

Bodyrags cling to me.
How could you sieve
so much sludge
through unbroken skin

and be repelled
by a life of slime?
You grasp a bramble:
African farmer

and Wyoming lady
resolve their bet.
One wins. The other chooses
a date on the calendar

to oppress me. Us.
And here I am
becoming fish.
Here I am

Letting old rivers
of salt bed me,
unable to change
for the wedding.

Lines, Ancient & Modern

Maurice V.'s Dido

1

"Over the bulwark into the sea
that's where fair Dido [1] has transported me."
But we soon moved on from that, boys
at the Grammar School, taking cue
from Maurice V. – not The Fifth, not King
of St. Caesare [2], despite his titles, just the sharp turn
of our year & first to call her Dido, our Queen
some years divorced from the Latin class
(urbem quam statuo, vestra est; subducite naves [3]).

She was Queen of France to those ignorant
of Carthage, daughter of Maas Charlie who lost
face and partner in Guadeloupe and prospered his charge,
not yet Queen, torment of our dreams,
on an estate he overseered or owned
with family settled abroad. There were grown men about
who swore 'Princess' Miss Geraldine was worth
bobbing on the Montserrat ferry this way
piled with provisions, that way with goats and live chickens
for . . . *Dido herself, splendidly beautiful* . . .

though not yet *widow,* married
or *giving way to frailty* as we think,
except as token for a quick boy
soon to leave the island on high tide of scholarship.

So we were willing fodder for Maurice V.,
old *heathens* from Coderington, skilled
at defying the adults, parents, aunts
on Sundays and in hot dreams escaping from our pants.

2

So boys, says Maurice V. wearing his crown
as "Village Idiot"[4], a title volunteered
to old Mister J. who asked one day in Physics
about professions after school expecting the usual
Doctor, Lawyer... Nurse, maybe – Got to be serious now:
we can't go give her majesty fair arms
except to complicate this business of colour.
Got to set an example here, to show those bitches in power[5].
After that, 'fair' Dido seemed too *period* for this reign
even to dull boys in 5b agreeing out of shame.
(So that's why I going board she like pirate: *bam*).
. . . Most desired ship in our harbour, Dido,
the Lady[6] who promised transport
to Medicine, the Law and other foreign spoil,
finds a boy rude against her waterline... These words
are ladders in the stocking of her frailty
gaining us the decks... *Now:*
Most desired ship in our harbour, Dido . . .

So what you think? Maurice V. asks as Ivan
and Pewter and Everton[7] playing cool now the real Everton
has toured and spent the afternoon coaching –
What you think? he asks
one night at Sturge Park[8] after the match
where we were beaten by some country team literal
about games; and we all agreed, advisors now,
that with the power of diction,
with a scholar fierce enough to dig up ground
when passing water, and with more than Virgil
and Shakespeare to rifle for language – the *bulwark*[9]
image which he coined after hooking
that boy for six and losing the ball, reflected
browsing browsing, man – and with *us*
to keep the metaphors smashing back and forth, "stocking

of her frailty", nothing special: our nerve holding,
Maurice V. stood chance with the overseer's daughter
where others – from ancient Libya & Tyre[10]
and now the blue-jacket man from Hither Gaul[11] –
failed; failed bad enough to *bawl*.

3

All who had failed, failed here.
St. Caesare, spread out, was a map of the world's
battlefields, from ancient to modern to now.
Last week's Irishman from the sea minus a hand[12]: what made
him so generous to fish with bait that had caressed
maybe foreign, cool and freckled women in lace
but *sickness* for our grape-coloured Geraldine?
On Sundays, squaring up to hymns long learnt, uncles,
more by courtesy than blood, surviving Panama
and Haiti showed breaches in the mouth, no trap
for Geraldine, a 'dentist' harder to please than all Trujillo's
henchmen, armed with parsley[13]
teaching foreigners a lesson in pronunciation
on the massacre river that night in '37
demanding your life for your accent. Survived to mock
neat stanzas like schoolboy graffiti in the margin
of the hymnal, of bats with human organs, the wife of *X*
bubbling rudeness to old Mister J., 'pallid' as the shade of Sychaeus
– parsleytenors seem to shout: with these flares she'll see us.
(I can hear them: *And with these flares she'll see us . . .*)

Agnosco veteris vestigia flammae[14] . . .
But the Queen was not a night-scholar
in this language gone stale in our climate:
you know what going happen if I not careful?
she asked her suitor, granting him a drink
he'd never tasted, letters behind his name, foreign
travel (he wished she had a loyal sister to act
as prologue or else, saving her, cue his play).
He proclaimed her soulmate not needing
him to be best at this or that, just sharpest
at the commentary, 'bed-pressing', boy (you so fresh
& *rysche*[15]) like no mere text-
book swot but a *browser* with wit

58

to counter Ivan's height and Pewter's claims
to family letters going back beyond grandparents
(handwriting legible, spelling good): he quelled
his fear that she saw *through* him
a stranger in a jacket made to sail
ships to fly planes, rich in imported
je ne sais quoi lines from Racine, Molière,
a few bars of Piaf . . . would this suffice for indifferent
gods – like Messrs. Wesley & De Lawrence[16] – to see him through?

To woo or not, like a tailor or seamstress, on his knees,
was the question: how else to match lips
to lips that were too knowing? He would bribe
the gardener, groom, whatever, the stand-in Punic Noble;
cram the names of flowers new to love:
how right this clematis matched her present mood!
Dido herself, splendidly beautiful, purple-hued,
(wilful enough to flirt the old school uniform, hair tied up in braids)
was saying to Maurice V.:

So you want to make
soup with me, dasheenman[17], is what you take
me for? maybe you just hate
me deepdown, eh? . . . like you
come come rumour[18] me, you want
to put hoe in my hand . . . or cutlass, maybe: you men
are all the same; why you don't go spray your energy
in foreign bush where your mind is already,
and stop stinking up the ground? Relieved
to be a man, relieved that this was Geraldine still,
raw in the mouth and not some distant Colette
or Yvette raised, portcullis-like, in Paris
beyond yards of snow (though prune-coloured
language on a small island sentenced you to be prim
and tight in balance), Browser called up words

like *julep* and *juniper* and *blubber* to command, asked Miss G.
to say her piece again in the accents of a Zola
book the school had banned, a hint he was bursting to declare
hell and black passion from way beyond Latin and Shakespeare.

4

Once upon a time, long ago, not so long ago, tomorrow –
when the heat was upon you and you wanted it all,
a bitch a slut of any sex wearing luck and brazenness
like a disguise in the new setting (prickled
by the devout[19] who, in departing the island, put fire
to their homes, dowsed their language
to prohibit return . . .) – But no one wants stories
like this except, at best, to humour you.
The one about boarding that 60s train billed
to last a decade, though they didn't tell you that,
till the sound of *Corina Corina*[20] trailed off
as revellers slipped out along the way – this tale
is too well mourned by those who were barely there.
Left alone on a train slowly filling with threat,
as if spilling from your own reading matter:
daughters too tempting, unlike those you wished
to have; daughters, revolting, like those you feared
to have, and large, slow-moving boys reopening the question
of evolution. They are here to blast your train
in slogans from the revolution you no longer trust,
like your crowd, to age gracefully
(Dylan's Corina has grown up and Dido's impossible
son has replaced Dido's impossible husband).
Ashamed of mess, for this too-much like home,
you find yourself holding brush & pan,
working through the blame alphabet, the 'L's'
today – Lennon, Lumumba . . .
facing a partner you've never partnered, no whys
& whens, bucket & pail in the wake of children
righting the world, too busy to clean themselves:
your pennance (for being too long on the train)
is empty bottles, broken glass & used clothes;
you wash and mend the furniture, pay the bills
and repair damage to the neighbours. This man

discovering this woman at a better place might draw comfort
from old books, sermons, jokes revealing
sluts and bitches to selves you can live with.
But it's too soon to indulge what might have been,
to bore with *Once Upon a Time* . . . to play this scene . . .

5

No use complaining Dido was the prize
that slipped through fingers clutching
even now at second lives; for we are at the age
where it pays to be content, and Geraldine, intact,
her breast dry of tears, has taken to growing pumpkins
after the ball. (She protests
that this storing of her memory in attic
parts of the Great House not built
is evidence of self-abuse concealing rape.) Point
taken. And if she's a widow now we can't
be suitors, can't go on playing at being boys,
though as Maurice V., still the brightest, even though
the stroke was cruel to his profile, says:
what else are we, grey hairs and limbs too stiff
to hold small lives together, qualified for?
To enjoy this age of restoration, King back in palace,
gadgets unknown to any monarch
before our time, pets dining from luxury
of imported tins; we're kept sane by call them Court Jesters
shaming us to laugh out loud at jokes
dressed in our own disabilities: I lisp I snail, the world
grows silent; we can't eat what we like because mothers,
refusing to stay dead, don doctors' coats and frighten us
with something less spiteful than the devil.
". . . I'm writing to you from a place called home.
Yesterday, we chased a butterfly that had hurt
itself: our debate to kill or not delicate as Chekhov . . ."
But off-stage, the spoils of conquest are women and boys
who lightly bear our names, prolonging some outdoor sport
to amuse the crowd: *There she goes! Over the bulwark
into the sea.* "The life, the life", from an oldboy
never privileged to be "Village Idiot" in our time,
and took a different route to manhood, his scars benign now
like cared-for flesh, suggesting fresh vegetables in the ground,

unpolluted waters and no need to seek reparations
from this State, that partner: in this stage of bliss
the grass is green is green is green and questions
of why we settle into these parts
avoiding the secret heart of hearts
the places where we, as it were, do our farts,
are never answered. If, as they say, the lessening
of one faculty sharpens another, let's pretend
that little skeletons under the crocuses, too small
to disturb sleep except in gentle questionmarks,
cloud our waking – like that shadow on that leaf,
slowly stretching out a wing to moth the garden,
leaf and moth filling some of your gaps today
all these translated years since Sychaeus . . .
And Dido herself, splendidly beautiful . . .
And Dido herself, splendidly beautiful.

1 **Dido:** Queen of Carthage, encountered by Maurice V. in Virgil's *Aeneid*. Sychaeus is her dead husband.

2 **St. Caesare:** French-British island off the coast of Montserrat (invented). Coderington, not the capital of Barbuda, is the village from St. Caesare where Maurice V. and his friends, 'the *Heathens*', now at the Grammar School in Montserrat, come from. They are quite proud of their 'French' connection.

3 **urbem quam statuo, vestra est: subducite naves:** The city I build is yours; haul up your ships. (*Aeneid* bk I 1 573)

4 Maurice V.'s titles include "Village Idiot", "Browser", "Heathen".

5 **bitches in power:** the 'bitches' are likely to be men in positions of power or influence.

6 **Lady:** After the 'Lady' boats, Canadian liners which used to transport bananas from the islands in the '30s and '40s; but had passenger cabins and acquired an up-market reputation, particularly after they ceased trading.

7 **Everton:** Everton Weekes (with Frank Worrell and Clyde Walcott, the Three W's, batting geniuses for the West Indies)

8 **Sturge Park:** The main cricket ground/playing fields in Montserrat, just outside Plymouth.

9 **bulwark:** a 'book' word, beloved of Grammar School boys of the period; like 'period' and 'cohort'. Or Maurice V.'s Falstaffian 'bed-pressing' (Pt. 3). Although here he could claim the less coarse Virgilian intention. Cf. Dido, after the banquet with Aeneas, 'pressed her body on the couch he left'. (Or could he be showing off his 'browsing' *Henry IV*, Pt. 2 not being a set text that year?)

10 **Libya & Tyre:** Maurice V. is careful not to acknowledge that in Virgil, Dido also rejects the advances of 'Chieftains bred by the land of Africa.' (bk IV)

11 **Hither** (nearer or Cisalpine) **Gaul:** So called by the Romans to distinguish it from Transalpine (Nether) Gaul – the greater part of modern France, Belgium, together with parts of Germany, Switzerland and the Netherlands. Here, the speaker is showing off his acquaintanceship with Caesar's *Gallic Wars,* when all he wants to say is 'Frenchman'.

12   In Montserrat (and hence, in St. Caesare) many of the fishermen of the period were descendants of Irish settlers. Accidents at sea were not unknown.

13   parsley… massacre: Story of an 'uncle', supposedly in Haiti, who found himself in the Dominican Republic at a bad time. Trujillo's army, tired of driving the immigrants back over the border, decided to kill them. To distinguish the French-speaking immigrants from the native Santo Dominicans, the soldiers held up sprigs of parsley to the suspects. Those who could say *perejil* (Spanish) were passed over. Those who said something approximating to *persil* (French) paid with their life. It is said that up to 30,000 died in that 'campaign' on the Massacre River (so named before the massacre) one weekend in 1937.

14   Agnosco veteris vestigia flammae: I recognise the signs of the old flame, of old desire (*Aeneid* bk IV 1 23)

15   fresh & *rysche:* colloquialisms (like *pouri* = thin or *pret-up* = rude/ saucy); *rysche* suggests the smell emanating from you after sex.

16   Wesley & De Lawrence: One, perpetrator of Methodism, the other, of esoteric knowledge, often invoked when 'Church' religion failed.

17   dasheenman: hint of the social hill Maurice V. has to climb. The poor, even if 'bright' were more likely to eat dasheen, tanya and breadfruit etc. rather than imported goods, meat. This, illogically, carried a vague hint of sexual 'strength'. (Maurice V. and the 'boys', also, weren't immune from snobbery. Cf. "beaten by some country team literal/about games" (Pt. 2).

18   rumour: In those days rumour took an evil joy
     At filling countrysides with whispers, whispers,
     Gossip of what was done, and never done
     (Aeneid)

19   devout: not in the narrow clerical sense; perhaps nearer to the sense in which one might link American 'fundamentalism' with the ethos of Hollywood. But these are just poor people, putting fire to their homes (many cases documented in Jamaica) prior to setting out abroad; they would allow themselves no bolt hole; they couldn't afford to fail.

20   Corina Corina: a Bob Dylan old favourite.

A Hundred Lines

1–20

"Something is broken inside my head"
Would be a good far-off line to end with
Though when I got there the damage might have spread
Though when I got there the damage might have spread
And the rest of me not know it.
Another false start, this, to the journey. "I must not cheat"
Is what brings me here, perhaps,
Set by an absent Master to fill pages
Till my nature blots the message
And wears it like a palmprint, reassuring,
Like others at a glance, yet darkly yours.
What have I learnt by repetition: I must not cheat,
Except to don the costume: I must not cheat,
At times, in places where dress is likely to be inspected?
And is this comfort enough to fill
The thimble of a cynic Master's dream?
But lines in detention are not questions,
Not moral issues, just irritants
Where, "I must not cheat. I must not talk in class",
Fall, like a cat's paw, on an indifferent page.

21–40

Lines, not sentences, he said:
So change the game and not squeeze sense
From a whim. Too clever to *J'accuse*
Men of the family who have tended to suffer early failure
Of the heart, etc. Settle for the safety
Of labourers outside mocking your fortune,
Hoes glinting, like teeth on edge, cutting corners
Like this
And this:
Inside, *patriam conservabit* (he will save the country):
Some such are sauntering towards release
While I pull at soil grown heavy: *J'accuse*
Le malheur des hommes[1]... etc. Nearer home, quote an ancestor,
Old tree, old stick from fruit long eaten, who never said it:
"More than good diet is required to restore heart
To men of the family . . . I will marry. Yes, I *will* marry".
Unconfident lines, a hundred times.
And see! My stomach is no spew of jealousy. No need to blame
The cook; to misdiagnose malice from the Home Physician
Till the voice breaks in a language not yet learnt.

41–60

In the country old women prepare
Your tin bath full of herbs and sickroom oils
To prevent your friends getting out of school ahead of you.
And now, to a later family, you cite that cause
And others, for this impotence,
Your page of pity, any man's palimpsest.
Tempt them with whiff of tarts baking in the stone oven,
Those young Sundays missed –
(You can see a messenger coming up the hill . . .
And recall an uncle's tales of abroad getting bolder)
The messenger, gone past the building, has nothing to report –
    except:
In England today 58 million items will be posted –
Who will add to this stock cluttering ground and air?
Dear Y, ... This 58th-million-&-*first* item can't bear the weight
    of its time. *Imagine* it.
So tell me again, uncle, of that night in Leeds, DC, Clapham
When, outnumbered, you saved the race . . .
Come back, family, with tarts from the stone oven.
It is said in another world you became a boxer
From rudeness, and got hit in the head;
And the tin bath with oils and herbs will save you from that.

61–80

an oho[2]

I'm lost in the forest
Of my ignorance: *oho*
Spilled the canejuice, lost the limes: *oho*
Far from *annato*[3] tree
To make me red and childlike
(My charms of axe and calabash in vain;
Spears and bows and arrows in vain): *oho*
O *maigok*[4], I am naked: *oho*
Great *piyaikma*[5], help me!
Oho

My voice is lighter than the wind
And makes no marks on your body: *oho*
My voice is smaller than your fear
Of *maigok* and *piyaikma*: *oho*
On my breath is canejuice *oho*
Fermenting inside (   )
Like a warning (   )
"Now all the dinners are cooked;
The plates and cups washed;
The children sent to school and gone out into the world[6]. . ." *oho*

81–100

lines culled from "Chief Seattle's 1854 reply"[7] to the offer
the "Great White Chief" in Washington made for a large
area of Indian land, promising "a reservation" for the
Indian people.

How can you buy or sell the sky, the warmth of the land? / Every
part of this earth is sacred to my people. / The perfumed flowers
are our sisters, / The deer, the horse, the great eagle, these
are our brothers. / If we sell you land, you must remember that
it is sacred; / That you must tell your children that it is sacred; /
That each ghostly reflection in the clear water of the lakes /
Tells of events and memories in the life of my people. / If we sell
you our land you must remember that the air is precious to us, /
That the air shares its spirit with all the life it supports. /
I have seen a thousand rotting buffalo on the prairie / Left by
a white man who shot them from a passing train; / If the beasts
were gone, man would die from a great loneliness of spirit. /
We do not understand / When the buffalo are all slaughtered, the wild
horse tamed, / The secret corners of the forest heavy with the scent
of many men, / And the view of the ripe hills blotted by talking
wires: / There is no quiet place in the white man's cities; /
No place to hear the unfurling of leaves in spring, or the rustle
of insects' wings: / What is there to life if a man cannot hear
the lonely cry of the wippoorwill or the arguments of frogs
around a pond at night? // The end of living and the beginning of survival.

1   Pascal, Pensées: "Le malheur des hommes vient . . . qui est de ne savoir pas demeurer en repos dans une chambre".

2   an **oho** (or oho-kari) is a special mode of expression used by the *Waiwais,* an Amerindian (Guyanese) clan for official announcements, formal requests and claims. Using short, fast, firm sentences, the speaker or *oho*-opener chants what he wants to tell his counter-claimant who, at the end of each sentence answers "oho", which can be translated as "yes", in the sense of "yes, I understand". The two participants in an *oho* sit on low stools opposite each other. The questioner invites the counter claimant to take a seat, and as each sentence ends, the adversary answers with a barely audible "oho". During the first stage, the opener flatters the adversary by speaking disparagingly about himself, etc. An *oho* can last from one or two hours to one recorded example lasting 26 hours.

In the present case the counter-claimant is a woman (the second half); and when she is seen to put her case, the claimant is clearly taken aback, and on occasion declines to answer *oho.*

3   **annato tree:** the red substance from the fruit of the annato tree is applied to faces and hands of travellers through the spirit-infested forest.

4   **maigok:** an evil spirit who lives in the forest and becomes invisible when he attacks.

5   **piyaikma:** a mountain spirit, the cause of sickness, epidemics.

6   **Virginia Woolf:** *A Room Of One's Own*

7   **Chief Seattle's Reply,** though a fake, was widely believed when it surfaced, and carried conviction. It still 'feels' right, even down to the rhetorical flashes.

Letter to Kate

When imprisoned, in 1979 for 'incitement and obstruction' i.e. for having been a founding member of Charter 77, Vaclav Havel was allowed to write one four-page letter to his wife, Olga [his only wife] under the following restrictions: 'No crossings out or corrections were allowed; no quotation marks, no underlinings or foreign expressions. "We could only write about 'family matters'. Humour was banned as well: punishment is a serious business, after all, and jokes would have undermined the gravity." '

I reach for your name and then think
Better of it, but I'm not allowed
Crossings-out, so you must stand, my love.
Let me explain, not who I am –
For this being a family letter,
You must know me – but why you have been
Reacquainted with this lover. I am,
As they say, distanced from a more familiar
Kate – not her name, you understand –
And must not use life's mishap to deny
Things their consequence: you cannot recouple
For a jailor's convenience. Kate, the name,
Is less foreign than Medbh or Tracy; sufficiently
Far from earlier family and not likely
To be suspected as a joke. Dear Kate,
Though apart, we must thank our luck
To be living at the same time in history,
And as one of us is not attuned to jokes,
The ban on this right, sorry, rite (emphasized
Not underlined) is not, indeed, onerous.
There are games that we like, separately,
And by rehearsing play at times fixed
By some public clock – a cockerel crowing-in
The day, or a blackout where I live –

We might win safe conduct for this letter.
Or the next. Carnal matters I dare not
Hint at publicly. I should lose you then,
And be claimed by some professional wife
With your name. My love, I count your lashes –
Sorry, no private joke of bedrooms,
Just the miniature fans that frame your eyes;
And no hint, truly, of the days crossed off my back.

To dance with Desmond Tutu

a toyi-toyi *on the occasion of Nelson Mandela's release from prison*

To say it's Sunday February 11th in the year of . . .
is to strain after effect, though the names
Winnie and Nelson must be circled on that calendar
which doesn't date. This draws it from the Headlines:
FALL OF CEAUSESCU. RELEASE OF MANDELA – and makes
it ours; not just the strobe of good news
that's been our reward these last few months
for being alive at this time. So spare a thought
for those dispossessed in the obit columns
on this day, Sunday February 11th in the year of . . . surprises.
Ten Thousand Days: 10,000 days and more in prison and he looks well
as if to check that cup of indignation short of the lips.
How to celebrate this and not tempt fate?
In the street they're dancing the *Tutu,* christened
after the Bishop. How to crash the party without
spoiling its rhythm? On the television a switch
of musicals blasts Rock for the Ambulancemen. Rock for Romania.
But I flex – fearful of the icon becoming flesh, slow-
moving in its newness, fearful for Winnie, mother,
grandmother, the nation's, the voyeurs' bride – I flex
through the prison of my own inhibitions
to join the Bishop in his element –
to dance in the street with Desmond Tutu
to dance in the street with Desmond Tutu
to dance in the street with Desmond Tutu . . .

Far from Jo'burg, no VIVA MANDELA T-shirt to merge
me with crowd, steps learnt from a lame grandmother
no match for the Bishop – *Tutu* – dancing to unite
families without end, filling space – 27 years wide,

generations-wide – till we can see no gap between lives, between partners;
dancing for those who must guard the house – *Tutu*
– dancing the *Tutu* for Biko, dancing the *Tutu* for Biko . . .
Praise poet, praise singer & I – stepping through the curfew of certainty,
testing the shift of gravity; defying guns, denying the cynics, breaking
from a prison of inhibitions
to dance in the street with Desmond Tutu
to dance in the street with Desmond Tutu . . .

War Casualty

Perez de Cuellar on his last-minute failed mission to Saddam Hussein:
"You know, I like to dance; but you need two to tango, and I didn't find
a nice lady."
Jonathan Dimbleby's heavy cold: puffy, hoarse, squinting eyes, gave the
appearance of someone who had emerged from an underground bomb-shelter.
His guests in the London studio seemed not to mind contamination.

Beside the All-seeing Eye whose maps
of the desert update the weather chart,
a portrait of Saddam, the Hollywood scud
tipped to run for President, too macho still
to tango with Mr. Perez de Cuellar
saddened that the nice lady's moustache
loses votes. But listen, listen,
the voice is hoarse, torn by war or sand;
this is Day Four of the war: is our man cracking?
Arrogant of translation, he assumes English, product

of those schools, one of us, almost.
The baddy puts on a soft young face
of debauchery, the BBC son, a Dimbleby boy croaking
us through war. "We've got now Colonel
Youcob from Kuwait, fighting for his studio.
Colonel Youcob, pay no attention to the germs
I release into air. My throat, raw
with sand and sympathy, aches to serve – a little
like you, Sir (My brother, on the other channel,
cannot relieve me). THIS IS AN EMERGENCY."

2
The Hugo Poems

Here we go again

She sat for days in the posture of prayer,
With eyes closed could see leaves returning
To the trees, birds restoring harmony to the island;
And two weeks on they say to her, we say to her:
Open your eyes and see leaves returning to the trees,
Birds restoring harmony to the island.
And she's afraid, she's afraid . . .

And here we are again, Brothers and Sisters . . .
Three weeks after Hugo [1] she can hear the piano:
She knows the sounds of this house, the old days
From kitchen, from animal pound, from washing-trough,
She was part of the music that kept it safe,
And we, cut off from those sounds console her,
Accompany her: *Yeah, I just found joy . . .*

She's in shock, off her head confusing
The washing of sheets in the old house
With her daughter's laundering in the new bank:
I just found joy . . . trickle of leaves . . . Yeah . . .
We're just poor people
On this patch of ground in Harris', gathered
O Lord, on a storm-damaged morning . . . *I just found joy . . .*

Was here in '24
Was here in '28
Will be here the day Soufrière
Vomit corruption back in we face.
Will be here for the Fire, the Flood . . .
. . . Just found joy I'm as happy as . . .

Another week: this isle is full of noises . . .

Emergency generators coughing like birds, farting, backfiring like birds . . .
And the Red Cross and books in the Library
To bring harmony back to the island . . .
And Persian carpets from our walls in Highgate,
And grandparents sitting again on the front verandah
To bring harmony back to the island . . . *Just found joy* . . .

Preachers, Preachers[2]

A grandfather's voice was mocked in this village –
(not his message, dear family, the voice, the *voice*).
A father's sermon corrupted by flesh
and by being filtered through a son's idiom, failed also
to release a note that the island trapped in silence.
Quarantined by sea not user-friendly, Montserrat
nailed down its speech under prim verandahs, disowned
syllables brawling in the marketplace. Ancestors brushing
up on language feared the cussing, the badword, the *cuciamout*[3]
bowelling at intervals, flood and blitz on an erring people.
In-between times we revert to good behaviour, send sons
(and daughters, now) abroad to seek lost words
for that sudden rainbow after the storm, for the arch
of flight from a childhood house that bats made,
lost to us now, with the house. Meanwhile preachers preach
around our fears: who will unlock the old voices trapped here?
Once, in childhood, I tried to free them from twin-pillars
looming, like something from the Bible, above our house
in Harris'. I failed. Friendly bees and guineafowl
cemented them to sky, to earth, with honey, with eggs.
Here's another stone, ancestor-like, squatting like a god.
Stripped by Hugo of cover, on this road above a bridge
where the murdered woman brought fever, for months, to my nights
too long ago – the bridge from Bethel whose Methodist church
alone among the Temples survived '28 – its mouth
open, like a cave we revisit despite tamer vows,
I become its audience, willing member of the congregation.
I hear it now, the lost hymn, the muffled howl;
I hear the deep, mock-laughter so much older than us.
It woke to Hugo, rumbled a profane song
whose notes broke not just glasses and promises granted on our knees,
but the backs of homes and churches, the order of our lives.

He was there, too, this clone, Preacher, when the rock said:
"To obey is better than sacrifice." The man's hands are still red.
". . . If gold and silver have to be tried by fire,
what say you to your soul which is more precious
than silver and gold?" He keeps the storm going,
three weeks late, this conduit to heaven and back, butchering
on his doorstep today, a lamb to shore up imagery.
This squat, sculptured, riot of muscle, this triumph
of pork, this Abraham confessing to be Bride of Christ,
is conscience given licence at times like this.
Other voices – party-politricks, details
of rematch between science and *myth,* the relabelling
of churches, banks – pale in description of our nakedness.
The soft pornographers, likewise, multi-
disciplined new men of travel and finesse, good
with the children, intimate spouses, clever, playful,
tuneful: SUCH BIG ERUPTIONS, GIRLS AWAKEN
              NO QUESTIONS ASKED BUT PRISONERS TAKEN . . . fail
to fill the mouth left bare on the hill. They do not keep faith
with Hugo, as this stained Messenger who swaps speech
for pronouncement: "Prepare ye the way of the Lord . . . Make
His path straight." Already he has disciples. The island
is his parish. And those of us, uneasy, who fail to find voice
between hurricanes, must bow to the storm that blows:
"I am the Blood of the Lamb. I am the Bride of Christ."

Major Browne's Library, Montserrat

Here I am in a strange place.
Here I am between the rock and a hard place,
my name sandwiched by *The Irish Phrase Book*
& BELFAST: *An Illustrated Architectural Guide.*
This would be a new passage of discovery
if books bearing your name had weight of the clan's
memory to survive a vandal pitiless
with wind and rain. The book, exiled here in Ulster,
sought anchor in Major Browne's private library [4]
which won't be unruined by new brick, new stone.

It looks untouched, so does the camera lie.
On the scene, I reached aimlessly for a book
newer than Thucydides, more solid than stapled
conference speeches: it refused to budge.
Burton's *Anatomy of Melancholy* welded itself
to wood, to *The Complete Plays of Bernard Shaw.*
Wordbricks of Psychology, Archeology, Greek
Political Theory and Education set into
one discipline, as if possessors of old *talk*
still played the power game: First
into Third Worlds won't go. These secrets,
like virgins, are preserved for those who stumbled
on them first. Shelf after shelf
joins this strike of knowledge; row
after row colludes. The Spanish classics;
Pascal, too, Zola and other saucy *livre de poche*
temptations, tease us. So that how it go.

But I have to tell you Sir, Madam,
we're no safer than Virgil, Juvenal, Young
Pliny and other old ruins. Our own books

grow mildew – and after such a short time
of being new! – like something forceripe,
bred of guilt. Elevation to the company
of Mr. *LammingNaipaulWalcottMittelholzer*,
one solid brick, fissured, like other fault-
lines running through this house, 14 years old –
opens up a sense of grievance for life-
in-progress too soon dignified.

Dora Browne (it's her library, too, her home),
teacher, linguist, like her husband, kept faith
during the raid, reciting stray verses
whose secular need and beauty ring true
after the event. Her thoughts were not of libraries:
when it was over, she was sane. Now we try
to rescue 'food parcels', 'remittances', 'Aid',
from an earlier, cruder dictionary
brought back for use in emergency. But it's too soon.
In the picture, Vincent, the Major (brown
shorts, T-shirt) looks out, puzzled: neat rows
of *Encyclopedia* behind his head contain nothing
he wishes to know. In complicity I accompany him
into the wreck of earlier times, '56
and my own house hurricaned for England:
there, an elder brother bragged snatches of French
learnt from Major Browne, that brought forth France
on our map of the world in Harris'. Now misshapen
Diderot, Abbe Prévost, Stendhal (none of them
childhood treats) make me hint at common loss.
But Brother Browne is out of reach, his gaze
seems further off, farther back.

The Boston Public Library was opened in 1854
And anyone who knows this fact is a bore.
Gracelyn, the island Archivist, puts paper
napkins between her pages; I think of pressed
flowers, joke of *Alexandria, Nineveh* and other
great libraries and the illustrious
ancients who tended them – what would the young
Ramesis have done about this Sam Selvon?
I resist, lift the public mask. Underneath, lament
for lost drawing-rooms of a few houses
where books – some not yet written – brought wits
out on a precious afternoon rescued
from Sunday School, to preen. Here, agnostic
headmaster and pious grandmother pitting book
against family lore to explain happenings
in the village confused, delighted us. Now, after
Hugo, Vincent and I hesitate to break
silence: scribbler and collector, civilians
in a war. Here we are, again, in a strange place.
Here we are between the rock and a hard place.

Kevin's Message to Montserrat[5]

I'm in between certainties: here they call me
A man with an Irish accent. I'm the legend
Who set foot on your Emerald Isle in the 1630s,
Did a bit of this and that, built Trecillian House
(Damaged, I know, but still standing) and courted
My first wife under the evergreen tree in Plymouth.
The church I built among temples of the Christians: how is it?

I suspect the committee naming your hurricanes
To be bureaucrats unschooled in our history. Hugo
Seems an odd policeman, a pre-Enlightenment pirate
Of the wrong tribe. Ah, you're not interested in this.
(Distribute your aid; give thanks to the Red Cross).
Here in Fun City, I wait by my car, clamped
By a rascal among the sex-labs to discredit me.

My thoughts, fellow-gamblers, are with you
From indigo, lime-grove to cashing in the chips. As you know
I have an interest in a bank on the island, off-shore
(No cumbersome buildings like churches to tempt God).
From North, East, Cork Hill, Kinsale, we must pool
Our assets. I'm coming soon to celebrate with the little
Hamilton girl. Tell she I love she.

Hugo Fallout[6]

On a clear day when the elements allow
you can hear the babel of rebuilding
on Montserrat, our neighbours rushing
headlong to restore status quo
as if Hugo hadn't given pause
to rethink. Here, in St. Caesare, behind
God's back, our roads cluttered, roofs
not yet restored to proud villas
they call us backwater, convict us in jokes.
Foreign helpers departed, their food
and medicines ripe for controversy,
we sneak time to re-invent ourselves
as others tut tut for folk
still dazed from the *trashing*. This man Hugo,
like a thousand, thousand husbands, fathers raining
blows down on their women, called forth
confession of wrongdoing which in turn
made him mad. Saviour or devil? Natural
to pause now and think what we think.
We indulge the walking-wounded
who talk well of the batterer; they are mad.
Others dredge for selves ill-hidden
under donated clothes. Will new rules
of fashion give these spasms of daring
a shape? The names of things that insult us
flood the mind like a vision: poet and prisoner
pleading second chance at a tree chopped up
at the roadside, at sighting the first *oriole*[7]
after the storm. Missing time, the chorus
of *sandpipers*[8] said to be extinct like village
carpenters gone abroad. For descant
preachers (O, think of tailors letting out,

of PE teachers and body muscle) straining
imagery to make things fit. O, says LQJ[9],
It's war, war among the rebels. But
across the water Montserrat forges
Will onto rock, the tattoo of hammer and nail
coming from villas no longer open to the sky.

Notes on *The Hugo Poems*

1   On September 17th, 1989, hurricane Hugo devastated many islands in the Caribbean and parts of the North American coast. Montserrat was the most severely hit with a dozen people killed, 90% of the property damaged and vegetation destroyed, some feared, beyond recovery. Hugo joined the hurricanes of folk memory '24 & '28, as something of a war which had been overcome, one effect of which was suddenly to have generated what is now seen as a Montserratian 'school' of writing.

2   **Preachers, Preachers:** one consequence of Hugo was the encouragement of fundamentalist kerbside preachers. Markham's father, grandfather & uncle were also preachers.

3   cuciamout: a sobriquet for acacia mouth.

4   **Major Browne's private library:** a photograph in the hurricane book *Hugo Versus Montserrat* shows a resigned Major Browne posing in a corner of his wrecked library. The bookcase, which looks suspiciously intact, proved, on investigation, to be ruined.

5   **Kevin's Message to Montserrat:** Montserrat is the Irish island in the Caribbean, having been colonized by Irish settlers in the 1630s – hence the Irish/Celtic placenames, surnames which survive to this day. After the hurricane many world leaders sent messages of support or sympathy to the people of Montserrat. Hence, an imagined one from Kevin.

6   **Hugo Fallout:** Montserrat seen from a St. Caesare perspective.

7   **Oriole:** the Montserrat *oriole,* commonly known as the *Tannia Bird,* is Montserrat's 'national bird'.

8   **Sandpiper:** the Spotted Sandpiper was another bird found in Montserrat before Hugo.

9   **LQJ:** Linton Kwesi Johnson; quote from his poem *Five Nights Bleeding*.

E.A. MARKHAM, born on the West Indian island of Montserrat in 1939, has lived mainly in Britain and other parts of Europe since the mid-1950s. His early plays, stories and poems reflect an unusually peripatetic life, a result of which are his poetry performances over four continents. A graduate in English and Philosophy, Markham taught widely in Britain/ Europe, returning to the Caribbean in 1970-71 to direct the *Caribbean Theatre Workshop*. From 1972-74 he was a member of the *Cooperative Ouvrière du Bâtiment* restoring houses in the South of France. Subsequently, he held a couple of Writing Fellowships in England, had a spell Media Coordinating in Papua New Guinea (1983-85) and returned to France in 1987 to do his 'Year in Provence'.

From 1988-91 Markham was writer-in-residence at the University of Ulster, and edited the literary magazine *Writing Ulster*. He has been involved in editing *Ambit* and *Artrage* magazines, and now edits *Sheffield Thursday*. He also organises the annual, international *Sheffield Thursday* poetry and short story competitions. E. A. Markham is senior lecturer in Creative Writing at Sheffield Hallam University.